Acknowledgments

God is my partner; his creations are our bounty. He has helped me to nourish our souls through my love of food and the people who share it at our table. Thanks to my family, Nelin Ahamed, the staff and all the guests at Sami's, whose inspiration and great palates have led me to write these soulful recipes. Words fail me in expressing my gratitude to all the talented people who volunteered their services and valuable knowledge to make things happen — so I'll have to cook you dinner! My sincere thanks to Neil Amsler for helping me finish this collection; besides being a wonderful human being, he is also a fine editor. Thanks to Ian Kim for capturing the essence of the moment through the window of his camera.

Of the many people who offered assistance and information, I would like to particularly thank the following: Maureen Vicar, Mr. and Mrs. S. Karim, Michael Brodrick, Barbara Madani, Georgia Nichols, John Piffer, Jamie Maw, Jason Puddifoot, John and Diane Atkinson, the Greater Vancouver Food Bank, our kitchen and dining room team at Sami's, the Cookshop, Connie McCalla, Seyit Gokkaya and Salim Kesani. My sincere thanks to Friesens for their generous support in the printing of this cookbook. Without your help and valuable contributions, this book would simply not have been possible.

To all I offer my humble gratitude.
Sami Lalji

For my Dad,

Always the underdog and always giving; never gave up for as long as God let him live.

Contents

Introduction

With all due respect to chicken soup, curry is the soul food in our Indo-Canadian household. Curry stimulates the endorphins and charges the nerves. It releases an enticing aroma and adds an exotic flavour to foods.

When I first arrived here as a refugee from Uganda in 1972, I knew that food was a way to win friends and the hearts of Canadians. During a break at work, the topic might be a reprise of last night's hockey game, but it was the garlic spareribs from the Chinese restaurant around the corner that made it an event.

At a very early age I knew that my passion was food and cooking. My family played a big part in developing my fledgling talents in the food and restaurant business – catering and food stalls were our only source of income. What a great training ground to start a career. I recall saying to my grandmother – as only the young can – "Someday I shall do a great restaurant." And so it was natural that when Star Anise, my first restaurant, was presented with a prestigious award by *Gourmet Magazine* in 1996 I should dedicate it to my mentor, always by my side, my grandmother Sherbanu Karim.

The East Indian culture and its foods form the basis for my cooking, but I also feel fortunate to have worked with some of Vancouver's finest chefs and restaurateurs. I've seen many cuisines from around the world influence our own regional cooking. Thirty years ago a memorable evening might include a cremated steak and a baked potato accompanied by a whisky sour or pink lady; now our diminishing world allows us to enjoy many different flavours and tastes. Ingredients from distant places are never more than a day away.

Spices are the world's oldest commodities – even prompting Columbus's voyages to the new world. Increasingly, western foods are being flavoured by curries and spices that are the mainstay of my cooking. I use them to enhance flavours, without overwhelming the dish.

At Sami's we have a lot of fun putting together recipes that are healthy, tasty and creative. Balance is the key. The spice must gently promote (and never dominate) the flavour and texture of the primary ingredient, be it fish, fowl, beef or vegetable.

Most important to remember is that cooking comes from the heart and soul of each individual. I might take the same ingredients as you to the stovetop but each of us will prepare something entirely different. What you hold in your hands – this book of love and recipes – is simply your guide. You may already have acquired a palate that enjoys the spicy side of curries; like me, you may find it very addictive! When you use these recipes, please feel free to alter them to suit your taste. So go ahead – make my curry!

A Note about Wine and Beer

If ever there was a beverage custom-made for a curry dish, it is wine. A good wine transforms the cuisine and expands its flavours. Known as wine chutneys in the time of the Raj, there are many varieties that complement spiciness: Gewürztraminer, Pinot Gris, Semillon, Riesling, Pinot Blanc, Pinot Auxerois, Zinfandel and Pinot Noir. British Columbia has long been an exceptional producer of such wines. With the rise in popularity of ethnic and fusion foods on the West Coast, what better way to celebrate a meal than to have local wines performing their magic? Beers and ales have also always been great partners for curries and spicy foods, and many local brewers produce fine liquid gold to wash down the hotter curries.

Smoked Salmon Pakoras

Serves 6 to 8

¼ lb.	smoked salmon, thinly sliced	112 g
2	potatoes, boiled, peeled and diced	2
1	zucchini, finely grated	1
1	carrot, finely grated	1
1	red bell pepper, seeded and finely chopped	1
1 cup	cooked white beans or chickpeas	240 mL
1	jalapeño pepper, seeded and finely chopped	1
1 Tbsp.	finely chopped fresh ginger	15 mL
1	egg	1
1 cup	bread crumbs	240 mL
	salt and black pepper to taste	
1 Tbsp.	Sami's Curry Powder (page 83) or Madras curry powder	15 mL
2 Tbsp.	olive oil	30 mL

Preheat the oven to 350°F (175°C).

1. In a large mixing bowl, combine all ingredients except for olive oil. Gently fold until well mixed.

2. With your hands, form small round patties into desired size.

3. Heat oil over medium-high heat in a skillet and sauté pakoras until both sides are golden, 1 or 2 minutes a side. Transfer pakoras to oven and bake for 10 minutes.

Serve hot with Tamarind Coulis (page 82).

Beverage suggestions

• Hawthorne Mountain Chardonnay or other Chardonnay

• Vancouver Island Brewery Victoria Lager or other lager

• Virgin caesar

Ostrich Samosas in Won Ton Wrappers

Serves 6 to 8

½ cup	olive or vegetable oil	120 mL
1 lb.	ground ostrich meat	455 g
	(or ground beef or ground turkey)	
1	onion, finely chopped	1
1 tsp.	ground ginger	5 mL
2	green onions, chopped	2
¼ cup	chopped cilantro	60 mL
1	jalapeño pepper, finely chopped	1
¼ tsp.	ground cinnamon	1.2 mL
	salt and black pepper to taste	
1	2-oz. (57-g) package	1
	of square won ton wrappers	

1. In a sauté pan heat ¼ cup (60 mL) of the oil. Add ground meat, onion, ginger, green onions, cilantro and jalapeño. Cook over medium-high heat until meat loses its pink colour and onions soften.

2. Add cinnamon, salt and pepper. Cook 10 minutes on medium heat. Remove from heat and cool to room temperature.

3. Form meat mixture into little balls about 1 inch (2.5 cm) in diameter. Lay out won ton wrappers on your work surface. On each wrapper place a meatball. Rub edge of wrapper with a little water. Place another wrapper on top and seal edges by pressing firmly with your fingers, making a perfect little samosa.

4. Heat remaining oil in the sauté pan over medium heat. Add samosas and sear both sides until golden brown. Continue with remaining samosas.

Serve hot with Seasonal Fruit Chutney (page 80).

Beverage suggestions

- Sparkling mineral water with lime

- Vancouver Island Brewery Piper's Pale Ale or other pale ale

- Spanish cava

On a journey in this vast land, I experience oneness with the land. The highway seems to flow through me and out the rear-view mirror. The mountains move with me – merely changing their shape over the miles.

Clams, Mussels and Swimming Scallops in a Coconut Curry Broth

Serves 4 to 6

¼ cup	olive oil	60 mL
2	cloves garlic, minced	2
2	green onions, chopped	2
1	large tomato, chopped	1
1 tsp.	Sami's Curry Powder (page 83) or Madras curry powder	5 mL
	salt and black pepper to taste	
1 cup	coconut milk	240 mL
1 cup	fish stock or clam nectar	240 mL
¼ cup	chopped fresh cilantro	60 mL
1 lb.	swimming scallops in the shell	455 g
1 lb.	mussels in the shell, scrubbed and debearded	455 g
1 lb.	clams in the shell	455 g

1. In a large saucepan heat oil over medium-high heat. Add garlic, green onion and tomato and sauté for 5 to 7 minutes, or until soft.

2. Stir in curry powder, salt and pepper.

3. Add coconut milk, stock or nectar and cilantro. Cook for 5 minutes.

4. Add scallops, mussels and clams, stirring gently. Cover and cook for 5 minutes. Discard any shellfish that have not opened.

Serve in large soup bowls with naan bread.

Beverage suggestions

- Gray Monk Chardonnay Unwooded or other unwooded Chardonnay

- Okanagan Premium Pear Cider or other pear cider

- Sparkling mineral water with lime

I remember a middle-aged man wandering into my father's store. After much deliberation he selected a jar of mango pickles and a package of lentils. At the cash register, he was embarrassed to realize he had left his money at home. My father simply smiled and said, "Enjoy your curry and beans, I am sure to see you again with your wallet."

Seared Squid and Eggplant Drizzled with a Tamarind Coulis

Serves 4 to 6

4	small Japanese eggplants	4
2 Tbsp.	sesame oil	30 mL
2 Tbsp.	olive oil	30 mL
1 tsp.	ground ginger	5 mL
1 tsp.	soy sauce	5 mL
1	jalapeño pepper, finely chopped	1
2 lb.	baby squid, cleaned, tentacles and all*	900 g
¼ cup	finely chopped green onion	60 mL
2 tsp.	sesame seeds, black and white	10 mL
2 Tbsp.	Tamarind Coulis (page 82)	30 mL

* You can purchase squid already cleaned from fishmongers; be sure the quill (sometimes called the pen), a slim bone in the tail, has been removed before cooking.

1. Cut each eggplant in half, crosswise, then into four, lengthwise.

2. In a large bowl place 1 Tbsp. (15 mL) each of sesame and olive oil, the ginger, soy sauce and jalapeño pepper. Add squid and marinate for 1 hour in the refrigerator.

3. In a large skillet heat remaining oils over medium-high heat and sear eggplant and squid for 1½ minutes on each side, until just cooked through.

4. Put the squid tentacles in the centre of a round plate. Place squid bodies and eggplant around the centre like bicycle spokes. Garnish with green onion and sesame seeds. Drizzle with Tamarind Coulis.

Beverage suggestions

- Hester Creek Pinot Blanc
  or other Pinot Blanc

- Bowen Island Brewery Blonde Ale
  or other blonde ale

- Iced peach tea

*I sit watching a lone seal pup
swimming in the cold waters of
the bay. A chill westerly takes the
warmth from my face; the seal pup
looks up at me with his marble eyes.
For a moment, I am sure he feels
my chills, as I feel his dampness.
Then he is gone.*

Crab and Shrimp Masala Cakes

Serves 6

1 cup	peeled shrimp, left whole	240 mL
2 cups	crabmeat	475 mL
½ cup	mayonnaise	120 mL
3	green onions, coarsely chopped	3
1	egg	1
½ cup	finely ground bread crumbs	120 mL
1	onion, chopped	1
1 Tbsp.	Sami's Curry Powder (page 83) or Madras curry powder	15 mL
1 Tbsp.	fennel seeds	15 mL
¼ cup	chopped cilantro	60 mL
	salt and black pepper to taste	
¼ cup	olive oil	60 mL

Preheat the oven to 350°F (175°C).

1. In a large mixing bowl combine all ingredients except olive oil. Mix with your hands until well blended. Form into round patties about 3 inches (7.5 cm) in diameter. You should have about 6 patties.

2. In a non-stick skillet heat oil and sear cakes on both sides until brown. Remove to a baking sheet.

3. Place in oven and bake for 5 minutes.

Serve with Seasonal Fruit Chutney (page 80) and/or Tamarind Coulis (page 82)

Beverage suggestions

- Hawthorne Mountain Chardonnay Semillon or other Chardonnay Semillon

- Okanagan Spring Brewery Traditional Pilsner or other traditional Pilsner

- Ginger beer

Spiced Corn and Lentil Mulligatawny Soup

Serves 4 to 6

¼ cup	vegetable oil	60 mL
1	large onion, chopped	1
1	large carrot, chopped	1
2	stalks celery, chopped	2
1 tsp.	ground ginger	5 mL
3	fresh tomatoes	3
½ tsp.	ground turmeric	2.5 mL
½ tsp.	fennel seeds	2.5 mL
½ tsp.	ground cloves	2.5 mL
1 tsp.	ground coriander	5 mL
1 tsp.	ground cumin	5 mL
1 cup	corn kernels	240 mL
1 cup	cooked brown lentils	240 mL
8 cups	vegetable stock or water	2 L
2 dashes	hot pepper sauce	2 dashes
2 dashes	Worcestershire sauce	2 dashes
	salt and black pepper to taste	
	yogurt for garnish	

1. Heat oil in a large saucepan over medium-high heat. Sauté onion, carrot, celery, ginger and tomatoes until soft.

2. Add turmeric, fennel, cloves, coriander and cumin and cook for 3 to 5 minutes.

3. Add corn and lentils. Stir well. Add stock or water and simmer for 15 minutes.

4. In a food processor or blender purée the mixture until smooth. Add hot pepper sauce, Worcestershire sauce, and salt and pepper.

Serve hot, garnished with a dollop of yogurt.

Beverage suggestions

- Sparkling mineral water with lime
- Mango Lassi (page 78)
- Masala Chai (page 78), iced

Cooking from the heart and soul can produce the finest flavours. A visual creation causes the juices to flow; a picturesque dish prepared as if for a magazine cover, with its array of colours, excites the taste buds. Without heart, no dish can be called Soul Food.

Chilled Minted Mango and Fresh Ginger Soup

Serves 6 to 8

4 cups	water	950 mL
6	mangos, peeled	6
1 Tbsp.	finely puréed fresh ginger	15 mL
1	lime, juiced	1
1 Tbsp.	chopped fresh mint	15 mL
2 cups	skim milk	475 mL
¼ tsp.	ground nutmeg	1.2 mL
1½ cups	Aqua Libra or herbed spring water	360 mL
	mint sprigs for garnish	

1. Bring water to a boil. Blanch the peeled mangos for about 1 minute. Reserve blanching water. Slice mangos and discard pits.

2. Combine all ingredients, except reserved water and mint sprigs, in a blender and process until completely puréed.

3. Add enough blanching water to puréed mixture to achieve desired consistency. Make it as thick or thin as you like.

4. Refrigerate soup.

Serve chilled with a sprig of mint.

Beverage suggestions

- Sauterne

- Flavoured martini

- Cassis spritzer

A mango is like a mantra. Its unique colour touches our eyes, its flavour touches our tongues, its core holds life.

Grilled Heart of Romaine with Tandoori Dressing

Serves 4

1	egg yolk	1
1	clove garlic, peeled	1
½ cup	olive oil	120 mL
¼ cup	Tamarind Coulis (page 82)	60 mL
2 Tbsp.	yogurt	30 mL
2 Tbsp.	grainy honey mustard	30 mL
2 dashes	Worcestershire sauce	2 dashes
2 dashes	hot pepper sauce	2 dashes
2	heads romaine lettuce, cut in half	2
¼ cup	freshly grated Parmesan cheese	60 mL
1 cup	croutons	240 mL
2 Tbsp.	roasted pumpkin seeds	30 mL

1. In a blender, combine egg yolk, garlic, olive oil, coulis, yogurt, 1 Tbsp. (15 mL) mustard, Worcestershire sauce and hot pepper sauce. Blend until smooth. Set aside.

2. Lightly baste romaine with 1 Tbsp. (15 mL) mustard on both sides. On a hot grill or barbecue, grill romaine on both sides until leaves are slightly charred.

3. Place a wedge of romaine on a serving plate and pour dressing over as desired. Sprinkle with grated Parmesan, croutons and pumpkin seeds.

Serve immediately.

Beverage suggestions

- Mango-lime margarita

- Mango Lassi (page 78)

- Vancouver Island Brewery Victoria Lager or other lager

Indian Summer Salad with Caramelized Walnuts

Serves 4 to 6

1	head radicchio, leaves separated and left whole	1
1	head Belgian endive, leaves separated and left whole	1
½ cup	Caramelized Walnuts	120 mL
1 tsp.	finely minced fresh ginger	5 mL
1	pear, thinly sliced	1
1	mango, thinly sliced	1
¾ cup	Tamarind Coulis (page 82)	180 mL

1. In a large salad bowl, mix radicchio, endive, walnuts and ginger.

2. Toss salad gently and place on chilled plates. Garnish with slices of pear and mango.

3. Drizzle coulis on salad as desired.

Caramelized walnuts

½ cup	sugar	120 mL
½ cup	water	120 mL
½ cup	walnuts	120 mL

1. Combine sugar and water in a saucepan, and bring to a boil over high heat.

2. Cook until mixture starts to brown. Stir in walnuts and remove from heat.

3. Cool to room temperature.

4. Chop caramelized walnut clusters into desired size.

Beverage suggestions

- Sumac Ridge Blanc de Noirs or other Blanc de Noirs

- Indian sherry

- Mango Lassi (page 78)

Medley of Vegetable Katchumber

1	jicama, peeled and thinly sliced	1
1	Spanish onion, diced	1
6	radishes, thinly sliced	6
1	red bell pepper, thinly sliced	1
1 cup	shredded tender red cabbage	240 mL
1	tomato, sliced	1
1	jalapeño pepper, thinly sliced	1
2 Tbsp.	chopped fresh mint	30 mL
¼ cup	raisins	60 mL
¼ cup	Caramelized Walnuts (page 28)	60 mL
½ cup	Tamarind Coulis (page 82)	120 mL
	salt and black pepper to taste	

1. In a large bowl, combine all ingredients.

2. Toss gently. Serve as a side salad or to accompany dishes such as the Lentil and Bean Kitcheri (page 38), Mumbai Blackened Sea Bass (page 50) or Roasted Leg of Lamb with Fresh Mint and Cumin (page 62).

Beverage suggestions

- Spanish cava
- Iced ginger tea
- Mango Lassi (page 78)

British East Indian–Style Vegetable Kitcheri

Serves 6 to 8

½ cup	butter	120 mL
1 cup	corn kernels	240 mL
1 cup	diced carrots	240 mL
1 cup	chopped onions	240 mL
1 cup	chopped red bell pepper	240 mL
1 cup	chopped celery	240 mL
1	jalapeño pepper, finely chopped	1
2	cloves garlic, finely chopped	2
1 Tbsp.	finely chopped fresh ginger	15 mL
2 Tbsp.	ground cumin	30 mL
½ cup	finely chopped cilantro	120 mL
1	Spice Bag (page 84)	1
6 cups	vegetable stock or water	1.5 L
3 cups	basmati rice	720 mL
	salt and black pepper to taste	

1. In a large stockpot melt butter over medium heat. Add corn, carrots, onions, peppers, celery, jalapeño, garlic and ginger. Stir and cook for 5 minutes.

2. Add cumin, cilantro and spice bag and cook for a further 5 minutes.

3. Add vegetable stock or water and bring to a boil over high heat. Add rice and cook, uncovered, until excess water is boiled off.

4. Season with salt and pepper. Stir mixture before covering the pot with a tight lid. Turn temperature down to low and cook for 7 minutes. Remove spice bag.

Serve immediately. Seasonal Fruit Chutney (page 80) is the perfect condiment with this dish.

Beverage suggestions

- Calona Artist Series Fumé Blanc or other Fumé Blanc

- Okanagan Premium Crisp Apple Cider or other apple cider

- Masala Chai (page 78)

West Coast Gujarati Vegetable Stir-Fry

Serves 6 to 8

¼ cup	vegetable oil	60 mL
1	large onion, chopped	1
1	clove garlic, finely chopped	1
1 Tbsp.	finely chopped fresh ginger	15 mL
4	green onions, chopped	4
1	red bell pepper, chopped	1
6	shiitake mushrooms, chopped	6
1	carrot, thinly sliced	1
1	stalk celery, thinly sliced	1
20	sugar peas	20
1	small zucchini, thinly sliced	1
1	jalapeño pepper, thinly sliced	1
1 Tbsp.	Sami's Curry Powder (page 83) or Madras curry powder	15 mL
	pinch grated whole nutmeg	
1 cup	vegetable stock	240 mL
	salt and black pepper to taste	

1. Heat oil in a large wok over medium-high heat. Sauté onion, garlic and ginger for 1 minute. Add remaining ingredients, except for vegetable stock and salt and pepper.

2. Cook for about 5 minutes, stirring continually to prevent sticking.

3. Add vegetable stock. Stir and cook for another 3 to 5 minutes. Add salt and pepper.

Serve hot with noodles or basmati rice.

Beverage suggestions

- Saki

- Vancouver Island Brewery Piper's Pale Ale or other pale ale

- Ginger tea

Grilled Vegetables in Tandoori Mango Vinaigrette

Serves 4

4 tsp.	olive oil	20 mL
1	mango, peeled and pitted	1
¼ cup	balsamic vinegar	60 mL
1 cup	yogurt	240 ml
2 tsp.	finely chopped fresh ginger	10 mL
1 Tbsp.	Sami's Curry Powder (page 83) or Madras curry powder	15 mL
1	jalapeño pepper	1
2 Tbsp.	honey	30 mL
¾ cup	olive oil	180 mL
1	medium fennel bulb, blanched and cut into 4 wedges	1
2	medium zucchinis, cut in half lengthwise	2
2	medium Japanese eggplants, cut in half lengthwise	2
2	red bell peppers, cut in half lengthwise, and seeded	2
8	shiitake mushrooms	8
1	large Spanish onion, cut into 4 slices crosswise	1
2	medium corn on the cob, cut into half lengthwise	2
2	bulbs garlic, cloves separated and peeled	2
	salt and black pepper to taste	

1. Place 4 tsp. (20 mL) olive oil, mango, vinegar, yogurt, ginger, curry powder, jalapeño and honey in a blender and process until smooth. Set dressing aside.

2. To blanch fennel, bring water to a boil in a stockpot. Add the fennel and cook for 1 minute. Remove and rinse under cold water.

3. In a large salad bowl combine ¾ cup (180 mL) olive oil, zucchini, eggplant, bell peppers, mushrooms, onion, fennel, corn, garlic and salt and pepper. Marinate for 15 minutes, tossing occasionally so all vegetables are coated with oil.

4. Preheat the barbecue for 10 minutes, or until the grill is very hot. Remove vegetables from oil and grill on both sides until grill marks appear or until vegetables are cooked.

5. To serve, place grilled vegetables on a platter and drizzle with the dressing.

Beverage suggestions

- Gray Monk Rotberger Rosé or other rosé

- Lime margarita

- Blueberry spritzer

A seed nurtured under all the right conditions produces fruit ripened to its fullest. But does the seed's soul request these conditions, or is the seed predestined to fulfill its mission?

Lentil and Bean Kitcheri

Serves 4 to 6

1 cup	Moongidal lentils (see page 87)	240 mL
1 cup	split peas and lentils, mixed	240 mL
1 cup	pinto beans	240 mL
1 cup	chickpeas	240 mL
1 cup	orzo	240 mL
½ cup	clarified butter (page 44)	120 mL
1	large onion, chopped	1
2	cloves garlic, thinly sliced	2
1 tsp.	ground turmeric	5 mL
1 tsp.	ground cumin	5 mL
1	Spice Bag (page 84)	1
8 cups	vegetable stock or water	2 L
	salt and black pepper to taste	
1 cup	basmati rice	240 mL

1. Wash lentils, split peas, beans, chickpeas and orzo thoroughly. Place in a bowl, cover with water and allow to soak for 1 hour.

2. In a large stockpot heat clarified butter over medium-high heat and sauté onions and garlic until transparent and amber in colour. Add turmeric, cumin and spice bag and cook for another 3 minutes on high heat. Add stock or water and salt and pepper.

3. Bring mixture to a boil. Drain lentil mixture. Add lentil mixture and rice to the stockpot. Turn heat to medium and cover pot with a tight-fitting lid. Simmer for 25 to 30 minutes, until rice and lentils are cooked and all excess water has boiled off. Stir several times to prevent sticking. Remove spice bag.

Serve immediately.

Beverage suggestions

- Mission Hill Grand Reserve Pinot Noir or other Pinot Noir

- Granville Island Brewery Gastown Amber Ale or other amber ale

- Mango Lassi (page 78)

Sweet Bell Pepper Massalum

Serves 4 to 6

¼ cup	olive oil	60 mL
3	bell peppers, chopped (red, yellow, green)	3
1	large onion, chopped	1
1 tsp.	chopped garlic	5 mL
1 tsp.	chopped fresh ginger	5 mL
1 Tbsp.	Sami's Curry Powder (page 83) or Madras curry powder	15 mL
1 cup	tomato sauce	240 mL
¼ cup	chopped cilantro	60 mL
	salt and black pepper to taste	
¼ cup	freshly grated Parmesan cheese	60 mL

Preheat the oven to 375°F (190°C).

1. Heat oil in a large ovenproof skillet over medium-high heat, and sauté peppers and onion for about 3 minutes.

2. Add garlic, ginger and curry powder, and cook for 5 minutes.

3. Stir in tomato sauce, cilantro, salt and pepper.

4. Sprinkle with Parmesan cheese, place in oven and bake for 10 minutes.

Beverage suggestions

- Hawthorne Mountain Merlot
  or other Merlot

- Shaftebury Cream Ale
  or other cream ale

- Mango Lassi (page 78)

*Take a moment and ask the soul
what it wants from you. " Peace,"
says the soul in silence. Did you hear
that? Sorry – I'll catch it next time.
Soul is always talking, it's for us to
listen in silence.*

Pappadum Crusted Salmon

Serves 4

6	pappadums, finely crumbled, straight from the package	6
1 Tbsp.	Sami's Curry Powder (page 83) or Madras curry powder	15 mL
4	6-oz. (170-g) fillets of salmon	4
¼ cup	olive oil	60 mL

Preheat the oven to 350°F (175°C).

1. Toss crumbled pappadums with curry powder and spread out on a tray.

2. Dip each salmon fillet in crumb mixture and place on a tray.

3. Heat oil in a non-stick sauté pan over medium-high heat. Add crusted salmon fillets and sear both sides until light brown, 2 minutes per side.

4. Place salmon on a non-stick baking sheet. Place in oven and bake 5 to 7 minutes, until salmon just turns opaque.

5. Serve hot with Seasonal Fruit Chutney (page 80) or Medley of Vegetable Katchumber (page 30). Delicious served with seasonal greens and your choice of dressing.

Beverage suggestions

- Blue Mountain Pinot Blanc or other Pinot Blanc

- Okanagan Spring Brewery Premium Lager or other lager

- Warsteiner Premium Fresh De-alcoholized Beer or other de-alcoholized beer

Winter is harsh. Huddled in the warmth of our house, I observe the lone tree outside. I ask, is the soul in the roots or in the buds that are ready to burst? In a few weeks it will be in full bloom and the wind will comb through it, letting the sun describe its shadow on the earth as it dances.

Oyster Stew in a Red and Green Curry Broth

Serves 4 to 6

2 cups	all-purpose flour	475 mL
3 lb.	fresh shucked oysters	1.4 kg
½ cup	olive oil	120 mL
⅔ cup	clarified butter*	160 mL
1	shallot, finely chopped	1
1	large potato, peeled and cut into small cubes	1
1	stalk celery, finely chopped	1
1	each red chili pepper, jalapeño pepper, finely chopped	1
1	clove garlic, finely chopped	1
1 cup	corn kernels	240 mL
1 Tbsp.	each ground cumin, coriander, turmeric	15 mL
½ cup	finely chopped fresh dill	120 mL
10 cups	fish stock or clam nectar	2.5 L
	salt and black pepper to taste	

* Clarified butter is butter with the milk solids removed. It's best used for dishes cooked over moderately high heat. Over low heat, melt 1 lb. (455 g) butter in a small saucepan. Skim off the foam that rises to the surface. Pour the clear melted butter into a glass jar, leaving the milk solids that have settled to the bottom. Discard the milk solids. Clarified butter can be stored in a jar and refrigerated for several weeks.

1. Place flour in a large mixing bowl. Dip oysters in flour and pat gently to remove excess flour.

2. Heat oil in a large sauté pan over medium heat. Sauté oysters until brown. Remove and set aside on a plate.

3. Heat butter in a large saucepan over medium heat. Sauté shallot, potato, celery, chili and jalapeño peppers and garlic for 10 minutes, stirring occasionally.

4. Add corn, cumin, coriander, turmeric and dill. Cook for another 3 minutes, stirring the mixture well.

5. Add stock and salt and pepper and bring to a boil. Remove from heat and serve immediately.

Beverage suggestions

- Sumac Ridge Blanc de Noirs or other Blanc de Noirs

- Cartier Private Stock Sherry or other sherry

- Lemonade

Saffron-Scented Rice Cooked in Curried Seafood

Serves 4 to 6

½ cup	olive oil	120 ml
1	clove garlic, finely chopped	1
1	large onion, diced	1
1	cinnamon stick	1
	pinch saffron threads	
1 cup	fresh shelled peas	240 mL
2 Tbsp.	Sami's Curry Powder (page 83)	30 mL
	or Madras curry powder	
½ cup	finely chopped cilantro	120 mL
	salt and black pepper to taste	
1	jalapeño pepper, thinly sliced	1
6 cups	fish stock or clam nectar	1.5 mL
3 cups	basmati rice	720 mL
2 lb.	assorted seafood, your choice of salmon, cod, prawns, mussels, clams, squid	900 g

1. Heat oil in large stockpot over medium-high heat. Add garlic, onion, cinnamon stick and saffron and sauté for 3 minutes.

2. Add peas, curry powder, cilantro, salt and pepper, and jalapeño. Cook and stir well for a further 5 minutes over high heat.

3. Stir in fish stock or clam nectar, rice and seafood, and bring to a boil.

4. Cook until excess water has boiled off, about 5 minutes. Stir several times and cover with a tight lid. Reduce heat to low and cook covered for 7 to 10 minutes.

Serve immediately.

Beverage suggestions

- Lake Breeze Semillon or other Semillon

- Spanish cava

- Warsteiner Premium Fresh De-alcoholized Beer or other de-alcoholized beer

Prawn Tails in a Lime Curry with Diced Papaya

Serves 4 to 6

¼ lb.	butter	112 g
⅓ cup	olive oil	80 mL
½ cup	onion, finely chopped	120 mL
2	cloves garlic, minced	2
3 lb.	fresh shelled prawns	1.4 kg
1 tsp.	Sami's Curry Powder (page 83) or Madras curry powder	5 mL
1	jalapeño pepper, finely chopped	1
¼ cup	chopped fresh dill	60 mL
2	limes, juiced	2
1 cup	dry white wine	240 mL
½	papaya, diced	½
	salt and black pepper to taste	

1. Heat the butter and oil over medium-high heat in a large sauté pan. Add onion and garlic and cook until transparent.

2. Add prawns, curry powder, jalapeño and dill. Stir and cook for 2 minutes.

3. Squeeze lime juice into mixture, then add white wine. Bring to a boil.

4. Add papaya. Season with salt and pepper.

Serve with basmati rice.

Beverage suggestions

- Gehringer Private Reserve Riesling or other Riesling

- Bowen Island Brewery Blond Ale or other blond ale

- Sparkling mineral water with lime

Mumbai Blackened Sea Bass

Serves 4

1 tsp.	chili pepper flakes	5 mL
1 Tbsp.	fennel seeds	15 mL
1 Tbsp.	finely chopped fresh ginger	15 mL
2 Tbsp.	Sami's Curry Powder (page 83)	30 mL
	or Madras curry powder	
4	6-oz. (170-g) fillets sea bass,	4
	or halibut, salmon or skate	
2 Tbsp.	olive oil	30 mL
2 Tbsp.	butter	30 mL
2	grapefruits, juiced	2
1 cup	finely chopped cilantro	240 mL
	salt and black pepper to taste	

1. Combine chili flakes, fennel, ginger and curry powder in a bowl. Mix well and dip fillets in mixture until well coated. Pat gently to remove excess.

2. Heat oil over medium-high heat in a non-stick sauté pan. Sear fillets on both sides until well blackened. Remove to a pan and keep warm.

3. Discard excess oil from sauté pan. Add butter and bring to a foam on high heat. Add grapefruit juice, cilantro and salt and pepper.

4. Bring sauce to a boil. Add fish to pan and cook for 2 minutes.

Serve immediately. Medley of Vegetable Katchumber (page 30) is an excellent accompaniment.

Beverage suggestions

- Sumac Ridge Sauvignon Blanc or other Sauvignon Blanc

- Still rosé

- Lemon ginger spritzer

Sharing is another way of winning. After a lovingly prepared meal, we'll drink a toast to our companions.

Madras Curried Chicken

Serves 6 to 8

½ cup	olive oil	120 mL
2 lb.	skinless, boneless dark and white chicken pieces	900 g
1	large onion, diced	1
2	potatoes, peeled and cubed	2
2	cloves garlic, minced	2
1	red or green chili pepper, finely chopped	1
1 Tbsp.	finely chopped fresh ginger	15 mL
6	star anise	6
1 Tbsp.	ground turmeric	15 mL
2 Tbsp.	Sami's Curry Powder (page 83) or Madras curry powder	30 mL
1 cup	yogurt	240 mL
½ cup	raisins	120 mL
½ cup	finely chopped cilantro	120 mL
4 cups	chicken stock	950 mL
	salt and black pepper to taste	

1. Heat oil in a large stockpot over medium-high heat. Add chicken, onion, potatoes, garlic, chili pepper and ginger, and sauté for 10 minutes, stirring occasionally.

2. Add star anise, turmeric, curry powder, yogurt, raisins and cilantro. Cook for another 7 minutes, reducing the heat to medium.

3. Add chicken stock, salt and pepper and bring mixture to a boil. Cook for 10 minutes.

Enjoy with basmati rice or thin pasta noodles.

Beverage suggestions

- Hawthorne Mountain Gewurztraminer or other Gewurztraminer

- Okanagan Premium Crisp Apple Cider or other apple cider

- Virgin caesar

Madagascar Butter Chicken

Serves 4 to 6

¼ cup	olive oil	60 mL
2 Tbsp.	finely chopped fresh ginger	30 mL
2 cups	yogurt	475 mL
	pinch Garam Masala (page 85)	
1 Tbsp.	pink peppercorns	15 mL
2 lb.	skinless boneless chicken breast, cubed	900 g
1¼ cups	whipping cream	300 mL
6 Tbsp.	tomato purée	90 mL
4 cups	chicken stock	950 mL
1	jalapeño pepper, finely chopped	1
	pinch cayenne pepper	
2 Tbsp.	Sami's Curry Powder (page 83)	30 mL
	or Madras curry powder	
½ cup	chopped cilantro	120 mL
¾ cup	unsalted butter	180 mL
2 Tbsp.	sugar	30 mL
	salt and black pepper to taste	

Preheat the oven to 350°F (175°C).

1. Combine olive oil, ginger, yogurt, garam masala and peppercorns in a large bowl. Add chicken and stir to coat well. Marinate for 15 minutes.

2. Spread marinated chicken on a baking tray. Place in oven and bake for 15 minutes.

3. In a large stockpot combine whipping cream, tomato purée, chicken stock, jalapeño, cayenne pepper, curry powder and cilantro. Bring mixture to a boil and cook for 10 minutes over high heat.

4. Add baked chicken and butter to sauce, stirring gently. Add sugar, salt and pepper. Once butter is melted, stir mixture gently and serve immediately.

Basmati rice, naan and Medley of Vegetable Katchumber (page 30) are great accompaniments.

Beverage suggestions

- Gray Monk Chardonnay Unwooded or other unwooded Chardonnay

- Vancouver Island Brewery Victoria Lager or other lager

- Iced ginger tea

The loss of a loved one is felt in the heart, the mind and all that was shared in the memories. Does the soul miss its soul mate? On this plane we entertain such worries. But the soul holds forever the experience and love of its soul mate.

Mugalie Fried Chicken Steak

Serves 4

1 cup	yogurt	240 mL
1 Tbsp.	ground cumin	15 mL
1 Tbsp.	ground coriander	15 mL
1 Tbsp.	ground turmeric	15 mL
1 Tbsp.	paprika	15 mL
1	jalapeño pepper, finely chopped	1
	salt and black pepper to taste	
4	6-oz. (170-g) chicken breasts, with wing bones attached	4
2 cups	bread crumbs	475 mL
¾ cup	clarified butter (see page 44)	180 mL

Preheat the oven to 350°F (175°C).

1. Combine yogurt, cumin, coriander, turmeric, paprika, jalapeño and salt and pepper in a mixing bowl. Using a whisk, mix ingredients well.

2. Add chicken breasts and coat well. Set aside to marinate for 15 minutes.

3. Place bread crumbs in a large dish and coat chicken breasts with bread crumbs on all sides.

4. Heat butter in a heavy skillet over medium-high heat. Gently sear chicken breasts on both sides until golden brown.

5. Transfer chicken breasts to a baking pan and bake in oven for 25 minutes.

Serve with Seasonal Fruit Chutney (page 80).

Beverage suggestions

- Peller Estates Oakridge White Zinfandel or other White Zinfandel

- Okanagan Premium Peach Cider or other peach cider

- Virgin daiquiri

Take the time to experience your soul's greatest joys before the curtain comes down. Look at the view, don't just pass through it.

East Indian Spiced Roasted Game Hen

Serves 6

3	1-lb. (455-g) game hens, split in half	3
1 cup	yogurt	240 mL
1	Granny Smith apple, peeled and diced	1
1 tsp.	ground cumin	5 mL
1 tsp.	ground coriander	5 mL
1 tsp.	ground turmeric	5 mL
2	cloves garlic	2
1 cup	chopped cilantro	240 mL
½ cup	honey	120 mL
	salt and black pepper to taste	

Preheat the oven to 375°F (190°C).

1. Rinse game hens in cold water and pat dry.

2. Purée all remaining ingredients in a blender.

3. Place game hens in a large bowl with purée and marinate for 30 minutes.

4. Transfer marinated game hens to a heavy roasting pan, placing them split side down. Roast in oven for 30 minutes.

Serve with Medley of Vegetable Katchumber (page 30).

Beverage suggestions

- Peller Estates Oakridge Cabernet Sauvignon or other Cabernet Sauvignon

- Okanagan Premium Crisp Apple Cider or other apple cider

- Mango Lassi (page 78)

The freshest ingredients are melded with spices my grandmother used. The food is made in heaven – it only passes through my hands.

Coriander Scented Duck Confit

Serves 6

12	4-oz. (113-g) duck legs	12
2 Tbsp.	coriander seeds	30 mL
2 Tbsp.	rock salt	30 mL
2 Tbsp.	finely chopped orange rind	30 mL
2 Tbsp.	butter	30 mL
1 Tbsp.	ground coriander	15 mL
2 Tbsp.	finely chopped fresh ginger	30 mL
2 Tbsp.	honey	30 mL
	pinch ground nutmeg	
	pinch cayenne pepper	
1 cup	coconut milk	240 mL
1 cup	chicken stock	240 mL

Preheat the oven to 350°F (175°C).

1. Combine duck legs, coriander seeds, rock salt and orange rind in a large heavy pot. Cover and bake in oven for 1 hour.

2. Remove duck legs gently to a rack placed on a baking sheet. Rest for 10 minutes, allowing excess fat to drip away.

3. Heat butter on medium-high heat in a heavy skillet. Add coriander, ginger, honey, nutmeg and cayenne pepper. Cook for 3 minutes.

4. Add coconut milk and chicken stock. Bring to a boil and cook until sauce starts to reduce and thicken slightly.

To serve, arrange duck legs on a large platter and drizzle with sauce. Indian Summer Salad with Caramelized Walnuts (page 28) accompanies this dish well.

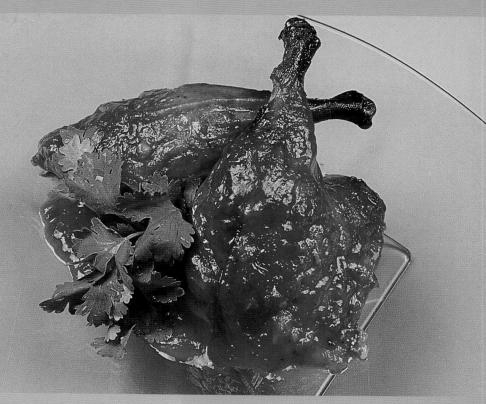

Beverage suggestions

- Cedar Creek Cabernet Merlot or other Cabernet Merlot

- Still rosé

- Orange spritzer

The most generous of gifts are unconditional – gifts from the soul. It is that unconditional giving that we know as kindness and love.

Roasted Leg of Lamb with Fresh Mint and Cumin

Serves 4 to 6

1	fresh whole leg of lamb	1
2 Tbsp.	olive oil	30 mL
2 Tbsp.	Dijon mustard	30 mL
2 Tbsp.	ground cumin	30 mL
1 cup	chopped fresh mint	240 mL
	salt and black pepper to taste	
	diced vegetables of your choice	
1 cup	veal stock*	240 mL
4 Tbsp.	balsamic vinegar	60 mL
1 tsp.	ground cumin	5 mL
2 Tbsp.	white or brown sugar	30 ml
1 cup	red wine	240 ml

* Veal stock can be purchased at specialty stores or can be made by boiling 1 lb. (455 g) of veal bones in 16 cups (4 L) of water in a large stockpot for 2 hours. Strain and discard the bones. Use as needed; the stock can be frozen for later use.

Preheat the oven to 350°F (175°C).

1. Trim fat from lamb leg. Combine oil and mustard and coat lamb with the mixture. Sprinkle with the 2 Tbsp. (30 mL) cumin, ½ cup of the mint and salt and pepper.

2. Place lamb leg on top of diced vegetables in a large roasting pan. Bake for 1½ hours, or until slightly pink in the middle.

3. Remove lamb from the oven and let sit for 10 minutes before carving.

4. Remove vegetables from pan and set aside. Deglaze the roasting pan with stock. Stir in balsamic vinegar, remaining mint, the 1 tsp. (5 mL) cumin, sugar and red wine. Simmer for a few minutes.

Carve the lamb thinly and serve on top of roasted vegetables with a light ladle of sauce.

Beverage suggestions

- Blue Mountain Pinot Noir or other Pinot Noir
- Still rosé
- Iced mint tea

Masaledar Lamb Osso Bucco

Serves 4 to 6

6	lamb shanks	6
1 cup	all-purpose flour	240 ml
1 cup	olive oil	240 mL
3	large ripe tomatoes, left whole and peeled	3
1	large onion, diced	1
3	stalks each celery and carrots, diced	3
3	cloves garlic, finely chopped	3
1	jalapeño pepper, finely chopped	1
1 cup	cilantro, finely chopped	240 mL
1	Spice Bag (page 84)	1
2 Tbsp.	Sami's Curry Powder (page 83) or Madras curry powder	30 mL
½ cup	tomato purée	120 mL
3 dashes	Worcestershire sauce	3 dashes
3 cups	dry red wine	720 mL
	salt and black pepper to taste	
1 Tbsp.	grated orange rind for garnish	15 mL

Preheat oven to 375°F (190°C).

1. Dust lamb shanks with flour.

2. Heat ½ cup (120 mL) of the oil in a large sauté pan over medium-high heat and brown lamb shanks on all sides. Place lamb in a large roasting pan.

3. Heat remaining oil in a large stockpot over medium-high heat. Add tomatoes, onion, celery, carrots, garlic and jalapeño. Cook on high heat for 10 minutes, stirring gently.

4. Add cilantro, spice bag, curry powder, tomato purée and Worcestershire sauce and cook for another 7 minutes.

5. Add red wine and bring mixture to a boil. Add salt and pepper.

6. Pour mixture over lamb shanks. Place in oven and bake for 60 minutes. Discard spice bag before serving. Garnish with grated orange rind.

Serve with basmati rice.

Beverage suggestions

- Peller Estates Oakridge Cabernet Sauvignon or other Cabernet Sauvignon

- Vancouver Island Brewery Piper's Pale Ale or other pale ale

- Virgin margarita

When an artist creates an uplifting image in thought, the soul is inspired and moved. When that image is brought to life, the work has the soul in its signature.

Kashmiri Beef Bourguignon

Serves 4

½ cup	vegetable oil	120 mL
2 lb.	lean sirloin stewing beef	900 g
3	large potatoes, cubed	3
3	stalks celery, chopped	3
3	each large onions and carrots, chopped	3
6	cloves garlic	6
3	large parsnips, chopped	3
1	Spice Bag (page 84)	1
1	jalapeño pepper, finely chopped	1
2 Tbsp.	Sami's Curry Powder (page 83) or Madras curry powder	30 mL
½ cup	cilantro, finely chopped	120 mL
2 Tbsp.	finely chopped fresh ginger	30 mL
	dash hot pepper sauce	
	dash Worcestershire sauce	
4 cups	dry red wine	950 mL
4 cups	veal stock (page 62)	950 mL
	salt and black pepper to taste	
	cilantro for garnish	

Preheat the oven to 350°F (175°C).

1. Place oil in a large ovenproof stockpot over medium-high heat. Add beef and sear in batches until brown on all sides.

2. Add potatoes, celery, onions, carrots, garlic, parsnips and spice bag. Cook mixture for 15 minutes on medium-high heat, stirring constantly.

3. Add jalapeño, curry powder, cilantro, ginger, hot pepper sauce and Worcestershire sauce. Cook for 5 minutes, stirring constantly.

4. Add red wine, stock, salt and pepper. Bring mixture to a boil.

5. Cover, place in the oven and bake for 1 hour.

Serve with naan bread and garnish with fresh cilantro.

Beverage suggestions

- Sumac Ridge Cabernet Sauvignon or other Cabernet Sauvignon
- Okanagan Spring Brewery Traditional Lager or other lager
- Cassis spritzer

Curried Crusted Calf's Liver in a Wine Sauce

Serves 4

2 Tbsp.	Sami's Curry powder (page 83) or Madras curry powder	30 mL
1 Tbsp.	Dijon mustard salt and black pepper to taste	15 mL
4	6-oz. (170-g) pieces of calf's liver	4
1 cup	cornmeal	240 mL
½ cup	olive oil	120 mL
1 cup	port	240 mL
2 Tbsp.	apple cider vinegar	30 mL
1 Tbsp.	pink, green or black peppercorns	15 mL

1. In a mixing bowl combine curry powder, Dijon mustard and salt and pepper. Add liver and marinate for 15 minutes.

2. Spread cornmeal on a tray. Dip liver strips in cornmeal, making sure they are well coated.

3. Heat oil in a heavy skillet over medium heat, and sear liver on both sides. Cook until golden brown (medium-rare), longer for well done.

4. Remove liver from skillet and place on a platter. Discard excess oil from skillet.

5. Add port, cider vinegar and peppercorns to skillet and deglaze on high heat. Cook for 3 minutes, until sauce starts to thicken.

6. Drizzle sauce over liver.

Serve with Seasonal Fruit Chutney (page 80).

Beverage suggestions

- Mission Hill Grand Reserve Pinot Noir or other Pinot Noir

- Vancouver Island Brewery Victoria Lager or other lager

- Aqua Libra or other herbal mineral water

Going back to Africa cleansed me. The smell of hot earth in the air before a tropical rainstorm touched a part of me that had felt empty for too long. I could hear my insides whispering: welcome home.

Sacred Porterhouse with Blueberry Coriander Jus

Serves 4

½ cup	balsamic vinegar	120 mL
1 cup	blueberries	240 mL
1 tsp.	ground coriander	5 mL
1 cup	veal stock (page 62)	240 mL
2 tsp.	sugar	10 mL
4 tsp.	Dijon mustard	20 mL
2 tsp.	ground coriander	10 mL
1 tsp.	cayenne pepper	5 mL
4 Tbsp.	olive oil	60 mL
2 lb.	porterhouse steak	900 g
	salt and black pepper to taste	

Preheat the oven to 350°F (175°C).

1. Place vinegar, blueberries, 1 tsp. (5 mL) coriander, stock and sugar in a small saucepan. Bring to a boil, and cook for 10 minutes, or until sauce starts to reduce. Set aside.

2. Whisk together mustard, 2 tsp. (10 mL) coriander, cayenne pepper and 2 Tbsp. (30 mL) of oil. Whisk to create a paste.

3. Rub paste on both sides of steak and season with salt and pepper.

4. In a heavy ovenproof skillet heat the remaining oil over high heat. Sear steak on both sides, locking in the juices.

5. Drain fat from pan. Return steak to pan, place in the oven and bake for 7 minutes (for medium to rare), or as desired. Serve with sauce.

Beverage suggestions

- Cedar Creek Pinot Noir or other Pinot Noir

- Hawthorne Mountain HMV Brut or other sparkling wine

- Sparkling mineral water with lime

Poached Mangos in Spiced Wine

Serves 6 to 8

1	Spice Bag (page 84)	1
1 cup	port	240 mL
1 cup	dry white wine	240 mL
6	mangos, peeled and sliced lengthwise	6
1 cup	sugar	240 mL
6 – 8	scoops vanilla ice cream	6 – 8
	fresh mint for garnish	

1. Place spice bag, port and white wine in a large pot and bring to a boil.

2. Add mangos and sugar and simmer for 5 minutes, or until mangos are soft.

3. Remove from heat and cool to room temperature. Refrigerate.

Serve this dish warm or cold with vanilla ice cream. Garnish with a sprig of fresh mint.

Beverage suggestions

- Sweet dessert wine

- Calona Sonata Port or other port

- Herbal tea

Maharaja's Khir Pudding

Serves 6 to 8

3 cups	milk	720 mL
3 cups	cooked rice	720 mL
1 cup	sugar, or to taste	240 mL
½ cup	sweetened condensed milk	120 mL
	pinch ground cardamom	
	pinch saffron threads	
¼ cup	chopped pistachios	60 mL
¼ cup	finely chopped dates	60 mL

1. Bring milk to a boil in a medium-sized saucepan over low heat.

2. Stir in rice, sugar, condensed milk, cardamom, saffron, pistachios and dates.

3. Cook for 10 minutes over low heat, stirring frequently.

Serve hot or cold.

Beverage suggestions

- Calona Sonata Port or other port

- Almond or hazelnut liqueur

- Masala Chai (page 78)

Banana Curry Flambé

Serves 6 to 8

1 cup	butter	240 mL
3	oranges	3
3	lemons	3
1 cup	sugar	240 mL
1 tsp.	Sami's Curry Powder (page 83) or Madras curry powder	5 mL
4	bananas	4
¼ cup	dark rum	60 mL
6 – 8	scoops vanilla ice cream	6 – 8

1. In a sauté pan heat butter over medium heat until it starts to foam.

2. Juice oranges and lemons. Add juice to butter. Toss the skins into the pan to steam flavour from them.

3. Add sugar and curry powder. Cook on low heat for 5 minutes. Remove orange and lemon skins.

4. Peel bananas and slice in half lengthwise. Add to pan. Cook for another 2 minutes.

5. Gently pour rum into mixture. Carefully light the alcohol just before serving.

Serve with a scoop of vanilla ice cream.

Beverage suggestions

- Paradise Ranch Chardonnay Ice Wine or other ice wine

- Masala Chai (page 78)

- Blueberry tea

It seems everyone in the room has a mate, from the very young to the very old. Why is there an empty space at my table? But memories of smiles and touch bring comfort. We miss a departed partner most on a joyful day.

Masala Chai

Serves 4 to 6

4 cups	water	940 mL
1	Spice Bag (page 84)	1
2 Tbsp.	sugar (optional)	30 mL
2 Tbsp.	loose Darjeeling tea (or 4 tea bags)	30 mL
4 cups	milk	940 mL

1. In a large saucepan bring water, spice bag and sugar, if desired, to a boil.

2. Add tea and milk and return to a boil.

3. Reduce heat and simmer for 5 minutes to allow the spices and tea to blend.

4. Strain chai into a teapot. Discard spice bag and tea leaves. If serving iced, let chai cool to room temperature and serve over ice cubes in a tall glass.

Mango Lassi

Serves 1 to 2

1½ cups	buttermilk	360 mL
1 cup	mango or passionfruit juice	240 mL
1	drop vanilla extract	1
	pinch ground cumin	

1. Combine all ingredients in a blender and purée until smooth.

2. Pour over ice cubes in a tall glass and enjoy.

Chai is now a global apéritif. In North America it is popular served over ice on hot summer days. It is said to be very calming for the soul and I wouldn't disagree, for chai always says to me, "Pull up a chair and take a load off your feet."

Seasonal Fruit Chutney

Makes 4 cups (1 L)

6	Granny Smith apples, peeled, seeded and diced	6
3	mangos, peeled and diced	3
1	large Spanish onion, diced	1
1	red bell pepper, diced	1
½ cup	dried apricots	120 mL
¼ cup	raisins	60 mL
2 Tbsp.	finely grated fresh ginger	30 mL
6	star anise	6
1	cinnamon stick	1
1 Tbsp.	Sami's Curry Powder (page 83) or Madras curry powder	15 mL
½ Tbsp.	cayenne pepper	7.5 mL
½ Tbsp.	salt	7.5 mL
1 cup	sugar	240 mL
1½ cups	apple cider vinegar	360 mL
1½ cups	freshly squeezed orange juice	360 mL

1. Combine all ingredients in a large saucepan and bring to a boil over high heat.

2. Cook mixture for 30 minutes, stirring occasionally to avoid sticking. Once excess liquid is reduced and chutney starts to thicken, turn heat to low. Continue to cook, stirring frequently, until thick.

3. Remove chutney from heat and cool. It will thicken as it cools. This chutney may be refrigerated for up to 6 weeks or frozen in small containers. Enjoy it with many of the recipes as a condiment.

Who would have thought the wine in the bottle might possess the soul of its grapes? Uncork the wine bottle, pour that soul in a dish that you are preparing for a loved one, and add your own soul and heart. Stir it well and comfort each other. Eat, drink and prosper!

Tamarind Coulis

1 lb.	dried tamarind	455 g
6 cups	water	1.5 L
6 Tbsp.	honey	90 mL
1 Tbsp.	ground cumin	15 mL
1 Tbsp.	balsamic vinegar	15 mL
1 tsp.	cayenne pepper	5 mL
	salt to taste	

1. Place tamarind in a mixing bowl and cover with water. Soak for 1 hour.

2. Using your hands, press tamarind through a strainer, reserving liquid in a saucepan. Discard pulp.

3. Add honey, cumin, balsamic vinegar, cayenne pepper and salt to the tamarind liquid. Bring to a boil, then remove from heat immediately.

4. Cool mixture to room temperature. Tamarind coulis can be refrigerated for up to 6 weeks and used for salads and marinades.

Sami's Curry Powder

6	curry leaves, dried	6
2 Tbsp.	coriander seeds	30 mL
2 Tbsp.	cumin seeds	30 mL
1 Tbsp.	black peppercorns	15 mL
1 Tbsp.	mustard seeds	15 mL
10	dried chili flakes	10
1	cinnamon stick	1
12	whole cloves	12
2	star anise	2
1 Tbsp.	ground ginger	15 mL
1 Tbsp.	ground turmeric	15 mL

1. Dry-roast curry leaves, coriander, cumin, peppercorns, mustard, chilies, cinnamon stick, cloves and star anise over medium-high heat in a heavy skillet until they darken, stirring continuously to prevent sticking or burning.

2. Cool mixture to room temperature and grind to a powder in a grinder.

3. In a mixing bowl blend spices with ginger and turmeric.

This curry powder will keep for 3 to 6 months in an airtight jar. Those who enjoy spicier curries can increase the chili flakes and peppercorns.

Spice Bag

6	cardamom pods	6
1	cinnamon stick	1
3	star anise	3
6	whole cloves	6
1	whole nutmeg	1
10	black peppercorns	10

1. Lay out a 6- x 6-inch (15- x 15-cm) piece of cheesecloth.

2. Place spices in the centre of the cloth and tie into a knot, securing ingredients in the bag.

You can prepare several spice bags at a time and store in a plastic bag.

Garam Masala

6	cardamom pods	6
1	cinnamon stick	1
3	star anise	3
6	whole cloves	6
1	whole nutmeg	1
10	black peppercorns	10

1. Dry roast spices in a heavy skillet for 3 to 5 minutes. Remove from heat and cool to room temperature.

2. Remove seeds from the cardamom pods and discard the pods. Crack the nutmeg into smaller pieces. Transfer mixture to a grinder, and process until finely ground.

Can be stored in an airtight jar for up to 6 months.

Glossary

Coconut milk

Purchased by the can, coconut milk is found in supermarkets and Asian food stores. Once opened, it can be refrigerated for up to 24 hours when stored in a plastic or glass container.

Curry leaves

Curry leaves can be purchased fresh or dried in Asian food stores and some supermarkets.

Curry powder

If you are unable to make Sami's Curry Powder there are several types of curry available in most supermarkets and Indian food markets. For these recipes we suggest Madras – a popular yellow curry powder that is a little hotter and widely available.

Garam masala

The name means "hot spices." A combination of ground, dry-roasted spices. See our recommended recipe (page 85). Because of its pungent flavours and aromas, a pinch will go a long way.

Hot peppers

These peppers, uncontrollably hot, refuse to be tamed. Use them moderately. There are many fresh varieties available: serrano, jalapeño, Anaheim, Fresno, Scotch bonnet, poblano – all with different degrees of heat. Check produce and Asian food stores and see which are in season.

Hot pepper flakes

The flakes are made from crushed, dried red chili peppers and can be substituted for fresh chili peppers. Widely available in supermarkets and Asian stores.

Hot pepper sauce

Many brand names are available in supermarkets and Asian food stores. Some, being very spicy, should be used moderately.

Jalapeño pepper

This spicy fresh pepper is widely available, year round, in supermarkets, produce stores and Asian food stores.

Moongidal lentils

This tiny, green, white-eyed variety of lentil is available in most Indian and health food stores.

Naan

This flat leavened bread is eaten with all Indian foods. Traditionally, naan is baked in clay ovens, or tandoors. In the home, it's baked in the oven or grilled. It can be found fresh in Indian bakeries and many supermarkets.

Pappadum	*Pappad* in India, this sun-dried, thin, crispy and spicy disc is made from chickpea flour. A great accompaniment with curries, pappadums are available at Indian markets and most supermarkets. Pappadum can be baked in the oven or deep-fried.
Peppercorns	Peppercorns can be black, white, green or pink. Black, the most common, is the dried, almost-ripe berry. White peppercorns are ripened berries with the dark outer coating removed. Green peppercorns are the unripe berries, usually preserved in brine. Pink peppercorns are not true peppercorns, but are from an entirely different plant. They are very aromatic and pungent. They are cultivated in Madagascar, hence their other name, Madagascar peppercorns. They are available dried or packed in brine or water, from supermarkets and specialty stores.
Saffron	Believed to be the world's most expensive spice, red saffron threads are sold in small, affordable quantities in fine food stores and some supermarkets. Fortunately, a few threads go a long way. Saffron powder is also available if the threads cannot be found.
Tamarind	Tamarind is a bean-shaped fruit available in Asian and Indian food stores. It is sold in a pod or dried with broken pods and pulp. It has the souring quality of citrus and is wonderful in marinades and with salads, meats, poultry and seafood.
Won ton wrappers	These thin pastry wraps are made of flour, eggs and salt. They are readily available in supermarkets and Asian food stores.

Shopping List

By stocking your pantry and refrigerator ahead of time, you will be able to make most of these recipes without having to search out too many ingredients.

Here is a short list of items to have on hand.

Fresh
cilantro
curry leaves
garlic
ginger
jalapeño pepper
naan
pappadum

Dried, canned or frozen
basmati rice
cardamom pods
chili pepper flakes
cinnamon sticks
coconut milk
coriander seeds
cumin
curry powder (Madras)
fennel seeds
lentils
nutmeg (whole)
pink peppercorns
saffron threads
star anise
turmeric
won ton wrappers

Index

Mugalie Fried Chicken Steak 56
Mumbai Blackened Sea Bass 50
Mushrooms, shiitake:
    West Coast Gujarati Vegetable
      Stir-Fry 34
    Grilled Vegetables in Tandoori Mango
      Vinaigrette 36
Mussels:
    Clams, Mussels and Swimming Scallops
      in a Coconut Curry Broth 16
    Saffron-Scented Rice Cooked in Curried
      Seafood 46

Naan 87

Orzo:
    Lentil and Bean Kitcheri 38
Ostrich Samosas in Won Ton
    Wrappers 14
Oyster Stew in a Red and Green Curry
    Broth 44

Pakoras:
    Smoked Salmon Pakoras 12
Papaya:
    Prawn Tails in a Lime Curry with Diced
      Papaya 48
Pappadum 88
    Pappadum Crusted Salmon 42
Parsnips:
    Kashmiri Beef Bourguignon 66
Pear:
    Indian Summer Salad with Caramelized
      Walnuts 28

Peas, green:
    Saffron-Scented Rice Cooked in Curried
      Seafood 46
Peas, split:
    Lentil and Bean Kitcheri 38
Peas, sugar:
    West Coast Gujarati Vegetable
      Stir-Fry 34
Peppercorns 88
Peppers, red bell:
    British East Indian–Style Vegetable
      Kitcheri 32
    Grilled Vegetables in a Tandoori Mango
      Vinaigrette 36
    Medley of Vegetable Katchumber 30
    Seasonal Fruit Chutney 80
    Smoked Salmon Pakora 12
    Sweet Bell Pepper Massalum 40
    West Coast Gujarati Vegetable
      Stir-Fry 34
Poached Mangos in Spiced Wine 72
Potatoes:
    Kashmiri Beef Bourguignon 66
    Madras Curried Chicken 52
    Smoked Salmon Pakoras 12
Prawns:
    Prawn Tails in a Lime Curry with Diced
      Papaya 48
    Saffron-Scented Rice Cooked in Curried
      Seafood 46

Radicchio:
    Indian Summer Salad with Caramelized
      Walnuts 28